Introduction

I0410034

Our journey began with a 125 gallon preformed pond in 1997 when we thought what a great addition to our landscaping and how much fun it would be to have a pond. Like most people just starting out, we had a vision of what we wanted. So we very strategically designed our layout, dug a hole, and found all the perfect rock to surround it. Now complete with the soothing sounds of water flowing and the thrill of watching the fish swim in their new home, for us that was the beginning of a passion that still continues to grow. Adding one pond after another; learning from trial and error, each and every time. With limited pond sources available in our area, we decided to share our love of water gardens with others. So WayCool Aquatics was established in 2008, offering an affordable way to purchase Koi, Comets, pond plants, and supplies. Turning into another great experience because of all the people we were able to meet. Realizing they have all the same questions, seeking all the same information we once did, led to the writing of this book in 2012. Even though this book is only recommendations and guidelines based on our own personal experiences, hopefully it will give you helpful information to make your pond experience easier, more enjoyable, and successful.

Over the years, a lot of people have asked my advice on how to take care of ponds, plants, and fish. I decided to put my knowledge and experience together to share with anyone and everyone that wants it. I'm hoping after reading this, you not only have what you need to care for your aquatic garden, but have even a bigger passion for all things great about being a pond enthusiast. I will try to cover everything you will need to know and that could take some time, so let's get started.

Let's start at the beginning, if you want plants and fish you must first have something to put them in. Although I am not going to cover how to build a pond but, more of what you need to make it work for you and what to expect. Whether you have a 100 gallon preformed pond or a 10,000 gallon liner pond there are four things you cannot do without and I cannot stress this enough!

Pump***Filter***UV light***Routine maintenance

And I repeat

Pump***Filter***UV light***Routine maintenance

Before you purchase your pond equipment you must first know how many gallons of water your equipment will be supporting. There are two ways to do this. The first is if you have just installed your pond before filling it, read your water meter, then read it again once full and calculating the difference of your readings will give you the exact amount of gallons of water your pond has. The other way is to measure the ponds width; length, and depth multiply the three figures to determine cubic feet. Then multiply that by 7.5 to get gallons. I have placed a pond reference guide at the back of the book to record this information, so it will always be conveniently on hand when you need it. When selecting a pump, the packaging will provide the gallon per hour rating (we will use 1000 gallon pond as an example). In order to get the results you're going to desire, purchase a pump that is rated substantially more than the actual gallons in your pond. In some situations, it's best to double the size of the pump (so in this case look for a 2000 gph pump).

If you don't, you will probably not be happy with the results. The reason for this is water circulation. It is best to circulate the entire volume of water in the pond every hour. When this is done more frequently, it improves the water quality in the pond. As with the pump, it is my recommendation, that the same be considered when purchasing a filter. Unlike the pump, filter packaging will have the recommended total gallons of the pond (i.e.-For ponds up to 1000 gal.). I would suggest buying a filter with the capabilities to support a pond of at least 1500 gallons if not 2000 gallons. Generally, the pump and filter should have the same capacity. I prefer a canister filter outside the pond. I believe they do a better job and they're easier to get to for cleaning. Many of them already have a built in UV light so you don't have to have two separate units. For smaller ponds, the submersible filters do ok. However they do sometimes require more than a weekly cleaning and they are much quicker to clean. The pump and filter are the heart of the pond. Here's some information every pond owner should know. This is where my past experiences can help you have more success without having to learn it for yourself. Where is your pump located in the pond? If your answer is on the bottom, do yourself a favor and move it. Place your pump on a crate, a brick, or cinder block, something to raise it off the bottom. The reason for this is, if you ever have a leak outside your pond which could be a hose that comes loose or water leaking outside a waterfall that has become clogged with debris; it can quickly empty your pond which could leave you with dead fish. I know this first hand. It was one of my worst experiences as a pond owner. I lost several fish just because we put the pump on the bottom of the pond.

The UV light, I thought was optional, but through my trial and error, you can save yourself the trouble of finding out the hard way. It's not optional, it is necessary if you want clear water. The UV light, like everything else, the bigger the better. 15 watt is my preference. There are other options though, for smaller ponds, a 9 watt would work fine. You will also need to replace your UV bulbs once a year to maintain its effectiveness. Even with the UV light working to fight algae, keep in mind if you have a pond, you're going to have algae. Like most pond owners, I try to keep mine under control which is why I do my yearly cleanout to have a fresh start with no algae. But then as the heat of the summer comes in, it's back. Dosing with Algae Fix keeps mine under control in conjunction with cleaning the filter weekly. I do have some algae that builds' up on my rocks and water fall. The only solution I have found to remove it effectively is pulling it off by hand, which doesn't take long.

Last but not least, routine, routine, and routine maintenance. If you want your pond to maintain a quality of clear water, algae control, and healthy fish, you must train yourself. Understand, you don't wait until you have green water or plants over growing there boundaries or fish that are dying before you worry about it. You will need to do weekly maintenance. This includes cleaning your filter, checking your pump for clogs, testing your water, netting any loose debris and dosing with an algaecide (I prefer Algeafix). If you only do it when you feel like it or only when you think you have time, you will possibly spend more time trying to fix problems than it would have taken you to perform 30 minutes to an hour of maintenance. Just to give you an idea, I have 8 ponds ranging from a 50 gallon preformed a 750 gallon in-ground to a 2200 above ground totalling 5000 gallons. I can perform my maintenance on all of them in an hour and half to two hours. So, pick a day of the week and a general time of day that you plan on investing an hour. Creating this habit is the most valuable thing you can do to ensure that you will enjoy your pond. Before we move on, what are the four main ingredients to an enjoyable, healthy pond? (If you can't answer this, you might want to read this section again).

Pump***Filter***UV light***Routine maintenance

Now that all the hard work is complete. It's full of water, the fountain and waterfall are sending out that all so peaceful sound, so your next plan is to run out and fill it with fish. Before you do, stop! Water works and leaks in mysterious ways plus it is full of chlorine and heavy metals. You definitely need to de-chlorinate your water before adding any fish. You will also need to de-chlorinate anytime you do a water change or just have to add water due to evaporation. More than that, I strongly suggest you start with putting some plants in and let your whole setup run for about two weeks. This will give you time to keep an eye on any problems that might arise before the risk of loosing fish and money. Make sure the pond is holding water and doesn't have any leaks anywhere. It will also give the pond a little time to become established. It takes a while for your filtermedia to gain the bacteria it needs for a healthy, stable environment for fish. If you just can't wait that long, try putting a few feeder fish (small comets) for the two week period just to be on the safe side. Whenever you decide to add fish, be sure your water has been de-chlorinated. I suggest Seachem Pond Prime. It treats many more gallons for the dosage than the majority of other brands on the market. It removes chlorine, chloramines, and detoxifies harmful ammonia and nitrite. It also provides essential ions and stimulates a natural slime coat beneficial for healthy fish. Be sure that you test or have your water tested before adding fish. If you are having any water problems, such as high ph levels or ammonia, do not add fish at this time. Get your water quality in check first or you will just be adding to your troubles and it will take longer to fix. If you're going to be a pond owner though, you will be doing yourself a favor by getting a test kit and doing it yourself. Not only do you learn a lot about what your water quality should be, over time you will recognize changes quicker which will allow you to diagnose, treat, and fix any problems much sooner. Low or high Ph is treated with a product called ph up or ph down. More of an issue is high ammonia, nitrite, and nitrate levels. These are treated with products that detoxify them, as a matter of fact, the pond prime I recommend, at a different dose, can also detoxify ammonia and nitrates, just another advantage of using it. You will also need to do water changes to help lower the levels if they are becoming high enough to affect your fish. This is why it's important to test regularly in order to catch it quickly. If you purchase a test kit, it will explain the correct levels and treatments in detail.

Quarantine fish

This is going to sound like a lot of trouble and many of you are not prepared to do so, but one sick fish can lead to many others. By keeping new fish quarantined for 7-14 days gives you time to keep an eye on any warning signs before introducing them to your existing fish. If you decide to do this you will need a separate holding tank. This can be anything that holds somewhere between 10-100 gallons of water (just depending on the quantity and size of fish you plan on adding to your pond). You will want to provide them with adequate aeration and if you have gone this far, I recommend salting the water to .3% level. If you see any signs of illness you would then want to medicate. I have put new fish in my pond without using the quarantine process and had some very bad results because of it. That is the main reason that fish sold at WayCool Aquatics have been put through the quarantine process before they are sold.

How to add fish

When bringing new fish home, you need to acclimate them before adding the fish to your pond. (If you have quarantined your fish as described above for your desired time period, you may omit this step). Plan on floating them for 10-15 minutes, at 5 minute intervals add a little water from your pond to their container. Using a thermometer will give you the most accurate way to know when to add them to your pond, by checking the temperature in the pond and in their container. When you have no more than a 2 degree difference (1 degree even better) net them from their container and release them into your pond. Discard the water from the container somewhere other than in your pond. If a thermometer is not available, the other option is to test the water with your hand, making sure the pond and container water feel very close in temperature. Your new fish may seem to hide when first added, but will soon come around. If possible, it is a good idea to add new fish right before feeding time. This allows the new fish a little time to swim around and get familiar with their surroundings without being harassed. Your other fish will be interested in eating.

How many fish is too many?

We have covered how and why water quality is so important. One of the major things that can impact that is the number of fish you have in your pond. How many is too many? Keeping in mind every pond is different due to water circulation, filtration, how often you feed, and the size of the fish makes a difference in how many fish you should have. Koi can grow up to three feet; obviously full grown they will need a lot of room. My experience tells me that more times than not, the koi's growth will adjust to the room they have. Meaning, instead of out growing the pond they just won't get as big. Comets and Shubunkin and other similar fish only get to a length of about one foot, once fully grown requiring much less space. If you have adequate filtration and circulation a guideline is 2" of fish per gallon of water. So, if you have a 100 gallon pond you can have up to 50" of fish (example 3-10" koi and 4-5" comets). The best thing to do is only add fish a few at a time then watch your pond closely, if you are not having any water quality problems and your fish seem happy then you're fine.

Season to season

At different times during the year, your pond may require different things. These things can differ for each person's setup, location, and weather. Keeping in mind I am located in Middle Tennessee. I have small and large ponds, some with surrounding trees and shade, others in sunlight all day (shade does help with the algae problems). In late summer or early fall, I net my ponds for two reasons, the obvious to keep leaves and debris out. The second reason is because as winter approaches, all the spring and summer life in our natural water ways is beginning to die off. Food is becoming scarce for wildlife, as this happens they begin to look elsewhere for food. The netting prevents the blue herring from getting their dinner from my Koi pond. This is also a good time to get ready for winter by removing any plants you may have that don't winterize in the pond and remove any UV bulbs so they don't bust. You may also want to be sure you have a pond heater on hand. Whether you shut your pond down, or leave it up and running year round, as I do, never allow the pond to completely cover with ice. In order to prevent harmful gasses from building under the ice surface, they need a place to escape. You can place a hot pot of water on the frozen surface, just enough to melt a hole in the ice, but with harsh winters you may have to do this many times. You can purchase an inexpensive electric heater that will do this job for you.

This is a Blue Herron just feet away from my koi pond.

Another thing I do that not all pond owners do, but it works for me, I do a yearly clean. When spring rolls around, I want a jump start enjoying the appearance of my ponds. After sitting all winter with the same water and no UV, I just feel they need a good cleaning. It also makes my routine maintenance easier because I am basically starting from scratch, which I find easier than trying to get them

back to where I want them a little at a time. I begin by checking the water temperature. I then lower the water level to make catching fish easier. As I remove them from the pond I transfer them to a small preformed pond or large storage tote that has been filled with water from the pond. Place the container in the shade with a small pump for circulation if you have one. If you don't have one, they will be fine for a while. It's a good idea to have an extra pump on hand, in case you ever do need to temporarily relocate your fish. Next, I pressure wash my liner, rocks, and plant pots using a sump pump to drain it. When I have drained all the water I can, I scoop up any remaining water or sludge with a dust pan and dump it in a bucket. Finally I use a very absorbent sponge and a bucket of fresh water to wipe up any other residue. You can begin refilling with water, being sure to add a de-chlorinator. This is where you need to pay close attention to your water temperature. It needs to be within one degree, no more than two of when you started in order not to shock your fish. If you need to adjust the water temperature, be sure you have it circulating. You may add buckets of hot or cold water depending on which way you need to adjust. Having the pond at least half full before returning fish, also allows you the option of adding water a little at time, over a couple of days avoiding the need to adjust the water temperature. While refilling, I use this time to clean the filter, put my UV bulb back in place, clean up and fertilize my plants. Now with a completely clean pond to enjoy all season, you can start your routine maintenance schedule from here. It sounds like a lot of work, I usually spend about 6 hrs on each of my large ponds, but for me, it's worth it.

Fish for your pond

This is definitely my favorite part of the pond, my koi are a little more like pets to me than just a fish to watch. I have standard Koi in one of my ponds and butterfly Koi in the other. This is where everyone gets to make their pond their own. One person purchasing Koi from me told me he always searches for the ugliest fish he can find. Some people like having catfish. Others absolutely adore that fantail comet. The best part of fish keeping; is the ability to choose one variety or several because they all do very well together. So don't be afraid to mix it up if that's what you like. The following is a list of fish that will do just fine if mixed in your pond.

Koi- My favorite and believe most of us have ponds to give these magnificent species a home as we enjoy there beauty. They provide the largest range of colors and patterns, Available in standard and butterfly.

Comet- Hardy and easy to care for. Colors vary from white, orange, red, or a combination of these. Available in standard and fan tails.

Shubunkin- Like the comet, very hardy, but also offers more of color variety adding blue and black to the comet colors. Available in standard and fan tails.

Fancy tail goldfish- A little less hardy than a comet and a little more inviting to predators because they swim slower but, enjoyed by many for their unique appearance.

Brim- I'm guessing this one comes in being inexpensive since you can catch them locally then release them in your pond.

Catfish- Not much in the way of color, they do offer size and will eat on algae. Some people love having them in there pond.

High finned shark- Very sensitive, but very interesting fish.

Mosquito fish- Small, but will consume algae, potentially disease carrying mosquito larva and other insect larvae.

Plecostomus- Not the prettiest fish, but will eat on algae. Will not tolerate winter conditions, need to be brought inside.

**WayCool
Aquatics**

Baby Koi

Foods to feed

Now that you have fish, what are you going to feed them? The market is saturated with the perfect food to feed any kind of fish. Some recommend different foods at different times of the season. I use Koi Vibrance stick food all season. It is great for hand feeding. My fish really seem to like it and after trying several different foods I prefer it. I start feeding my Koi when my water reaches 50 degrees. I only feed them once a day. If you want them to increase in size more quickly, you can feed twice a day. Any more than that and, I feel not only a waste of food, but now making the filter and UV light work harder than they really need to and the additional risk of poor water quality. What else can you feed your fish? I have heard a variety of things actually. Some of those being honeycomb cereal, cheerio's, lettuce, cucumber and many other things. I prefer giving mine sliced oranges. Although, I can't be certain, my research shows it's good for their color (my fish do have good color). I also like watching them. I had never seen a 20" Koi attack an orange slice before, but it is quite amusing. Just some snack ideas, but I wouldn't over do it. I have found no information on how much is too much, so I only do this about once a week. While we're on the topic of feeding fish, I will share with you how to train your fish to eat out of your hand. I started this to help engage my children in my hobby. The younger ones love it and now I get to share it with my first grandson.

You should begin by feeding your fish everyday at the same time. Select a location of your pond that will be easiest for you to access the water and where you have a good view. Place a handful of a stick type food in the water at the very edge of your selected location, place your hand in the water and leave it while the fish consume the food. If they seem reluctant or don't eat, that's ok. Leave your hand in the water for at least 2 minutes. Follow this every time you feed your fish until the majority of them will eat as soon as you drop in the food while leaving your hand in the water. Next step, hold the food with your hand closed, lower your hand in the water. When a few fish come close, release just a couple of pieces. When that has been eaten, release a few more until you have the majority of the fish realizing the food is coming from your hand.

Final step is to then place one piece of food between your fingers, lowering it into the water. Continue to hold it there until a fish tries to eat it, when they do release it. At this point you have successfully got your fish to eat out of your hand. Do this as many times as you have fish interested, when they loose interest feed as usual so they can consume what they need. You can leave your hand in the water if you wish; it will only reinforce the habit you're trying to teach them.

I have had many fish eat out of my hand over the years. It is well worth the effort and is really much simpler than it sounds. I do want to share some tips not outlined above because like people, every fish is different. By trying one or more of these tips you could have your fish eating out of your hand much quicker, a lot of it depends on them. So give them a try, if they don't prove productive, follow the specific outline above. It will work.

*Try placing one piece of food between your fingers, lowering it into the water. If they respond, continue feeding one piece at a time as long as you have fish interested, if this is successful you have completed the process and only need to continue reinforcing the habit.

*You can also hand feed several fish with an open hand approach instead of one piece at a time. With this you have hand fed fish, just not individually.

*Something else that can speed up the process is to put your fish in some kind of floating container which will give them limited area, once you have them eating out of your hand, put them back in the pond and follow the outline above.

Some people do not feed there fish unless they eat out of their hand during the training period. I never felt the need to cut there diet just to train them and it has always been successful for me.

I hope this brings you success and a new appreciation for your Koi, comets, and Shubunkin.

Small koi trying to eat from my hand

Fish treatment How do you know that your fish are sick? I can only give you what I know from my experiences and unfortunately, I have had a few different battles with this. If you have fish that you can physically see damage, such as red in there fins, spots or abrasions on there body that is easy, you know you have a problem. If you have fish at the top of the water gasping you may have a problem but, a little harder to diagnose. You have two main concerns, bacterial infections and parasites. If you suspect parasite, looking at the underside of the fish will show more symptoms than the topside of the fish. When I had problems, I sought advice from many different people with knowledge about ponds and fish. I want to express, it is a very difficult thing to diagnose and what to treat them for. Every minute of every day spent spinning your wheels, trying to figure it out, usually cost you more and more fish loss. I am not going to get into a lot of the details about specific dieses or parasites because it is not only lengthy, but you can find all this overwhelming information on line. Trust me, I have spent a lot of time trying to diagnose, but after all my years of doing this, I learned a way to fix the problems. I no longer try to figure out specifically what they are suffering from, but instead treat them early to avoid a catastrophe. On two different occasions I started loosing fish.   After revealing the symptoms, several people determined my fish were suffering from a bacterial infection, dosing them with one medication, then another and then another. The results I was getting were more and more dead fish every day and a lot of expense. I now have one solution to most every problem and not only has it worked for me, each and every time since I started using it, I have successfully helped other people avoid what I went through. At the first sign of any problem I test the water. If I do not have any water problems such as high ammonia or nitrite, I dose my pond with Tetra Fish Treatment which treats bacterial and parasite. I also salt the pond to a .30 level.

Medication- there are many different medications available for many different ailments, the Tetra Fish Treatment has given me the most reliable results and is harmless if dosed unnecessarily. As a preventive measure you can dose your pond in early spring which is the most likely time for fish diseases.

Salt treatment-some recommend salt to cure many external parasite and fungal infections, although I have not seen this specifically, I do believe it does help in their healing. It may also be used as a preventive measure. If you decide to continually salt your pond; I can save you some money. The pond salt you buy at the pet store is very expensive ($12.99 for 9 lbs); purchase a water softening salt ($5.00 for 40 lbs) instead. It does the same job and not only did I test its safety, I used it for several years in my pond. I have also treated sick fish with the same result of the pond salt. A salt level testing kit will be handy to have if you decide to salt your pond water or when dosing fish.

Plants

Plant varieties and options are even more abundant than fish; a blooming lily or lotus just brightens up the day no matter what color it is. The first couple of years I didn't have a lot of success with plants. I continued to try to learn more about them and get any advice I could. I bought several little starter plants, followed the instructions and they either didn't do anything or they sprouted then quickly died. I even tried some hyacinths how easy is that, still no success. At one point I just gave up. After purchasing an established potted lotus (because it was the most gorgeous thing I had ever seen) and a Lillie, my plant opinion completely changed. I do recommend buying an already establish potted plant, even if it cost you a little more, you will probably be much happier with the outcome.

Once established, plant care is really minimal. I fertilize my lily's and lotus once a month during the pond season, which is from late March early April to late September early October. I remove any dead foliage so it doesn't end up at the bottom of the pond and so the plant looks great. The following is a list of the more popular plants.

Cattail-easy to care for, blooming and non-blooming varieties.

Iris-easy to care for blooms early spring, variety of colors.

Lilly- great plant for shade requires fertilizing to get the most of flowering.

Cannas- easy to care for, many different varieties.

Lotus-Absolutely stunning plant offers dimension, shade, every pond should have one, fertilize monthly to get the most of flowering. It needs to be potted in a round solid pot.

The following floating plants do not require potting, they do not winter in my area so have to be replaced each year, but they multiply quickly.

Hyacinths- moderate to care for blooms purple flower.

Water lettuce-moderate to care for, do not flower.

Plant care

In early spring, everyone is ready for the hyacinths and lettuce. Because of the difference in weather, and the stress of being shipped, can affect how they do in your pond (I was always told, just throw them in and they will multiply like crazy). When purchased very early in the spring, to get the best results, I place them in a shaded area where fish can't get to them. Let them rest for a few days or until you are looking at a rich dark green and signs of a good healthy plant. Now they are ready to be put in your pond, but do realize fish love them. If your pond does not have an area inaccessible from the fish, you can place a few in a storage container or large bucket. Also dosing them with a liquid plant food increases the growing and blooming.

If you are planting or replanting plants for your pond I recommend yard dirt. Having tried the aquatic soils, I know how expensive they are, along with the mess. Honestly, the quality of my plants improved greatly when I changed to yard dirt (the more clay the better), once planted, cover it with rock. If you have larger koi use larger rock, because they will make a mess with pea gravel and possibly remove the plant from the pot. Spray it with a garden hose and pour the dirty water out. Then slowly lower it into the pond, you will probably still get a dusting of dirt but it will clear up quickly. Keep all your plants in containers.

Absolutely stunning lotus

You don't want them take over your pond. It will deprive the fish of the room and oxygen they need. When they start growing outside the pot, you need to remove what has escaped the pot. Or, you can re-pot it in a larger container, divide it, and only re-pot what you want. Any unwanted foliage can be cut back; generally speaking you care for your pond plants the same way you do your yard or garden plants.

This lily has out grown its pot and covered the entire pond surface.

We have covered a lot of information. So whether you are still thinking about installing a water garden or if you have had one for many years, I hope you have enjoyed reading this and gained some usefull knowledge.

My Pond Reference Guide

Pond measurements _____W_____L_____D

Gallons_____

	Purchase Date	Warranty Period	Replacement Date
Pump #1	_____	_____	_____
Pump #2	_____	_____	_____
Filter #1	_____	_____	_____
Filter #2	_____	_____	_____
UV #1	_____	_____	_____
UV #2	_____	_____	_____

Notes

Photo Gallery

Established lilly providing shade

Beautiful lotus flower

For this fountain my husband & I used an elephant ear leaf to create a concrete cast.

Custom built pond by my husband Todd Thornbury

Preformed ponds no digging required

WayCools pond Cleanouts

Before

After

Before

After

Young standard & butterfly koi

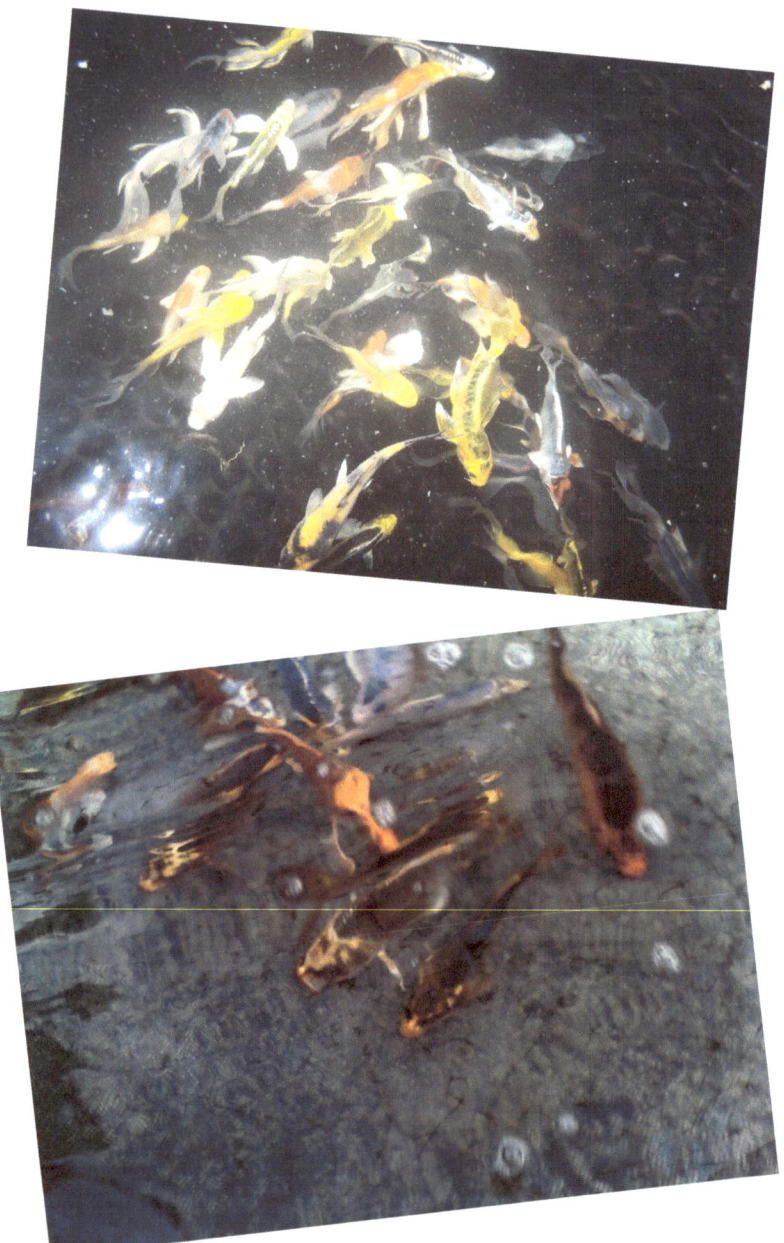

Koi captured with the reflection of moving water

WAYCOOL AQUATICS

615-289-1956 OR 615-394-2930
115 Jade Court, Rockvale TN 37153
WayCool Aquatics.com

You're Source for Koi, Pond Plants & Supplies
Pond Cleanouts***Special Orders

We hope if you have not visited WayCool Aquatics before,

you will.

And if you have visited us through the years we

Thank you!

www.ingramcontent.com/pod-product-compliance
Lightning Source LLC
Chambersburg PA
CBHW050925290526
45792CB00002B/891